Eylenda

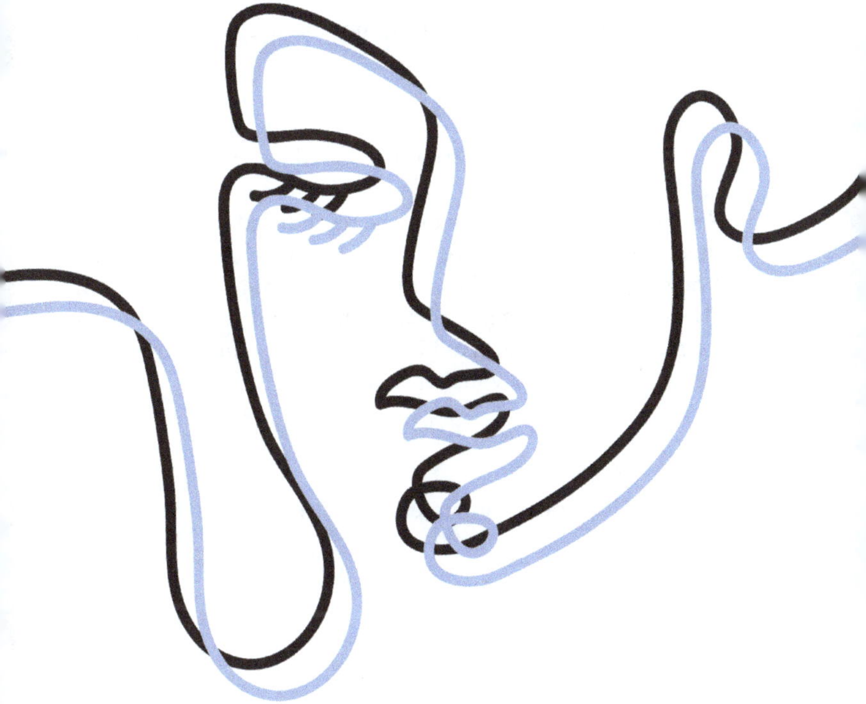

Aríel Bertelsen

First published in Great Britain in 2022 through IngramSpark

ISBN 978 1 3999 3218 9

This book is set to be published as part of a dissertation project for a master's course in Publishing from Kingston University.

To my glacial Jökulmær,

to my beautiful Fjalladrottning,

mín Hrímey,

to my brave Týli,

to my unwavering Norðurey,

kæra Eylendan mín.

Contents:

Emeralds, you know

Springs of green,

look up,

look up at me,

please.

Thanks.

Emeralds, you know,

emeralds and all

of those

old,

magic…

rocks.

No, not like the song,

Yes, like the

crystals,

you know,

rocks… *emeralds*.

No, listen.

Aríel Bertelsen

Like the

forgotten rocks.

You know, like,

olivine and peridot

and serpentine,

or malachite and adventurine

and vesuvianite.

Yes, olivine like olives,

and,

before you ask,

yes, olives like the

olive theory.

Oh, and peridot,

peridot is

your birthstone.

Wait– no,

nevermind,

it's the diamond.

I know that

diamonds 'aren't

even green',

I mixed them up.

Yes, I know

when your

birthday is...

May... oh,

it's emerald.

Your birthstone.

it's emerald.

Mine is sapphire–

whatever.

Then serpentine,

well, because you are

a snake...

as in houses,

like in Harry Potter.

Yes, I know

it's called Slytherin.

I am a Ravenclaw,

obviously.

Yes, I'm very

blue,

I'm aware...

it's the depression.

Then malachite,

because it sounds

like malakai.

No, not like

Malachai,

the Stephen King

character, but

malakai, as

in 'my angel'

in Hebrew.

So, adventurine.

Yes, adventurine like

adventure.

No, not like

when we

had sex on

the lifeguard chair.

More like

when we

did it

in the woods.

Okay,

maybe it is not as

exciting, but

it was more magical.

Magical as in–

whatever.

Vesuvianite.

Yes, like Mount

Vesuvius.

Yes, the volcano that

killed thousands of

people.

That's not the point.

I am trying to

compliment your

eyes.

As a romantic

gesture or

something,

I dunno.

Oh, I am not *that*

unromantic.

Because,

well,

because I

I can't say it back.

Say,

those words,

back.

So...

emeralds, you know.

Jökulmær

In the unbreathable heat,

my body racked a sob,

a cry.

A cry for home,

for something to feel like heim,

heima.

And somehow my own hands

dug you up from the earth,

a piece of home.

Green eyes shining with the speckled colours

of norðurljós.

Skin like snjófall and birch bark,

freckles of olivine.

Lips like newly picked blueberries

about to burst under your teeth,

coloured in lingonberries,

krækiber stained tongue.

I lay upon your thighs,

in your groin of pillowy moss.

And the moles that dot your body,

your chocolate marks,

I left there with my kisses.

I trail your body,

up,

upp.

At the back of your neck;

a white mark,

from a time when you laid

with an elf.

The nights you danced with them,

when you forgot your name,

I whispered it back.

The names you gave me,

the ones you changed.

A rose did not fit me.

Rather I should be a forget-me-not,

gleym-mér-ei,

because you would never forget me.

Now you whisper the same.

Humming along to Bubba

came like a rumble in your chest,

another earthquake in the warmth

of the earth.

Smoke floats out of your cracks,

into the cold loft,

but it is not reykur at all

but vapour

in your misnamed

Valley of Smoke.

Your sweet vapour strokes my

thighs with a wet kiss,

a paintbrush,

a blooming of poppies and pansies.

Your eyes catch me,

fiðringur up my stomach,

as a looming stone figure

atop your breast

stands guard.

I look up, past your mounds

your curves and his gaze,

to gorgeous Fjalladrottning mín.

My Jökulmær,

come to me in dreams.

Held in your embrace,

blueberries against my nape,

and with whimpers

my Norðurey's fingertips

grace my pearl.

Sjáumst,

in an airport,

next time it will be mine.

Sjáumst,

in a snow pile,

while you pick snjókorn out of my gold.

Hittumst,

in the corner of a bar,

á morgun if you would like.

Hittumst,

wherever you'd like.

The ballad of us

You speak

        and I speak.

I say

        and you say.

So you laugh

        and I snort.

And I giggle

        and you cackle.

Then you sigh

        and I hush.

I whisper

        and you whisper.

I gasp

        and you laugh.

So I shout

        and you scream.

You howl

        and I shush.

So you hush

        and I say.

I speak

        and you say.

You speak

        and I agree.

Then you kiss

        and I kiss.

And oh do you kiss

        and I yield.

I yield

        and you laugh.

You push

        and I gasp.

You chuckle

        and I muffle.

I lap

      and you let.

So I push

      and you play.

And you do

      and I 'stay'.

Then you hum

      and I hum.

I hum

      and you hum.

You hum

      and I hum.

You moan

      and I 'Oh Gods'.

You kiss

      and I hiss.

You laugh

      and I breathe.

I kiss

        and you nudge.

So I say

        and you 'That was fun'.

Petals

You weep

      weep,

weep your

        petals

onto the street,

onto the road.

Raining

      over the car,

the sad,

rusted

red.

Hailing

      over the road,

the sidewalk,

ground

grey.

Brown, pink, white

and gold,

all of you,

only you and

your petals.

The petals that

you weep,

weep.

The pressed down,

flat, bleeding

petals,

all over my feet.

And they fall,

they do.

They fall in my

hair, my

eyes, my

lips.

And I kiss,

     kiss

the petals

       away.

But they fall,

       they do.

They fall onto

me, into

me...

like you do.

Like you always do,

you weep,

      weep,

weep your

      petals.

Alfaðir

Black wings aflutter

underneath the light of Máni

and the ground rumbles at a whisper...

caw caw

I seem to remember now,

remember what I always somehow knew.

The wind whispered to me in dreams

of faraway and close lands,

it whispered of a tale

that once was yours and once was mine.

The earth sighed out in puffs

of great vapour, in gusts of magic,

spraying over my eyelids,

daring me to recall of times past and new.

The trees giggled behind my back,

shifting and hiding,

with murmurs of Freyr's name

to keep me checking and turning.

The rocks spoke among themselves,

as if nor I, or anyone, could hear them,

knocking out words

about us and the ones before us.

The waves shouted and screamed and screeched,

begging to be heard far above the land,

but no response ever came

worthy enough of answer.

The fire that emerged within me then,

brought me far off my feet,

above the wind, the earth, the trees, the rocks,

and the waves.

They pulled with all their might,

and from within the land sprouted ice.

As the fire diminished and the ice melted,

there came the light,

hanging from the black talons

of an unkindness of two.

They yielded and merged and separated,

landing me once more,

and each took their place,

one on my shoulder,

and the other one behind my head.

I closed my eyes and breathed in,

but when I opened them again,

the whispers, sighs, murmurs and screams

were no longer there.

The ravens had taken up their spot within me,

and the things I once saw, heard and felt,

the Alfaðir being me and him me,

were nothing more than forgotten

memories and dreams.

Into you

The dirt, damp and dark,

nestles under my

fingernails,

under the chipping, brown

polish.

It sticks in the creases

in *crescents*,

in bundles of earth.

My fingers drive

into the soil,

dig deep,

staining neatly

as they go.

The dirt crumbles off

and again I pry

the soil open,

dig deep.

I push my palms in

to feel grounded,

to feel the earth,

my earth.

Hands, to palms, to

forearms and arms.

It hugs my shoulders

and kisses at

my moles.

Swallows and caresses

my neck,

my nape.

Tangles in my hair

in knots and

bundles of earth.

I lay onto my back,

letting you dig into

my spine, into

my waist, into

me.

Toes and soles

bury down,

and my malleoli

melt and become

one with you.

You take a hold of

my hips and pull

and grind

and sway

into me.

And we dig and bury,

claw and nestle,

push and bundle,

swallow and pull,

tangle and kiss,

and melt.

Melt into you.

Aríel Bertelsen

Dirt over my buttons,

my breasts,

my bones.

Dripping into you,

into us,

and wink farewell

to the Sun.

That time

So, do you remember?

Do you remember that time?

That time, you know.

That time when we met.

Yeah, no, just checking...

Hm? What did I think?

Of you?

A lot.

I thought of you a lot.

I thought that you were absolutely-

Don't insult yourself like that.

Anyways, I was saying...

Absolutely stunning,

beautiful, gorgeous

and hilarious.

... You made me snort half a

shot of vodka

three minutes after that meeting.

It burned.

Thanks for asking.

Hm? Oh, right, that time.

I liked you...

right away.

I enjoyed you.

I thought that you wouldn't look my way.

I mean that I don't see myself

the way that you do.

And yes... you did.

You did look my way.

And yes, you do still look my way.

Back then,

in that time,

we were different.

Different from what we are

now.

Yes, you looked my way.

You had never looked

at a woman

in that way

at that time.

I was the first, you say.

That you caved,

you saw me,

and you caved,

you say.

You were also my first

in that way.

The first one to

make me think

'Yes, like this'.

Where was I going with this?

Oh, right, that time.

Oh, I knew,

at that time,

I knew.

Knew that you'd be mine.

that I'd be yours.

For you,

I knew,

always for you.

Týli

Waves shimmer and crash,

crash and shimmer around my calves,

the rocks and shells and seaglass clatter and tumble,

tumble and clatter around my grounded feet,

klakk, klakk, klakk.

The seafoam rises in tones of white and sage,

clinging to me, hanga,

dragging to me, draga,

pulling to me, toga,

calling in that sweet violet voice to come,

come home,

heim.

I reach out a hand, grasping for her,

fingers threading through the threshold of the thule

sea, sinking into the barrier of the world,

fingers to claws and fins and flippers,

reach.

A whispered song,

soft and airy, above and over the waves,

in hair rustles and wet skirts,

and a deep rumbling singing beneath,

from the earth and the rocks and the shells

and further down,

nether,

neðar,

niður.

They pull and call and I yield,

water barrier over inked skin,

past my elbow,

past my shoulder,

face pressed up to the door,

unknown and known blue eyes looking back.

The mirror of the sædrottning pressing a light kiss,

koss to my cheekbone,

fingers brushing over cool roundness.

Grabbing on, I retreat,

bidding farewell to fins and claws,

the cool encasing my middle finger

in a snug hug, knús.

I raise my hand flat to the sky,

bearing an Óðin's stone as a ring.

As I delicately take it off,

the sun shines through the hole

and down into my iris.

I let the sunlight follow down, placing the stone

upon my eye,

saltwater sliding down my face.

The day sky turns to dripping purples and pinks,

a swirling of azures and sapphire and teal –

the water bellow turns clear and aquamarine,

soulful hands grasping for my ankles,

singing whispers of Ísafold

and Hrímey

and Týli.

The wax and the flame

The flame sways

and fades

and brightens

with us.

As you twirl.

and swing

and lay

me around.

It flickers as you wink,

and rises as you kiss.

It falters as I whine,

and stops as I hush.

The flame licks at your

fingertips

and your tongue

laps up my flame.

And the wax

as you move

it clears

and rises

and sinks.

It trickles as you press,

and slowly as you nudge.

It drips as I waste,

and lands as I hum.

The flame burns.

It burns

and reddens

and swelters

and blazes

and sometimes it hurts,

hurts how it sways

and fades

and brightens–

Then the wax puddles

down where the heat pools,

and the flame and the wax form one

with us as we...

Molten fingers thread through

my golden ropes.

And the tiny lines of silk

catch at the tips

of lava, rock

and nails.

And you weave and

weave and weave,

arms of my hair

from the palm

to the elbow,

and again–

The tips curl up,

singe and twinge,

as you thread

and weave,

and they fall, snap,

right off.

And then a braid.

A fish of rope, silk,

and fire.

Molten curls of gold

and copper,

and bits of silver.

It jumps and flaps

and flails,

thrashing

and slapping.

You pull;

it unfurls.

Lock after rope

after silk

after yarn,

it unfurls

and loosens

and you let go.

And you undo and

undo and undo,

hair after skin

after flesh

after bone,

I come undone.

Eylenda

You call to me in dreams,

with whispers of an empty earth,

a fallen sky,

the hum of cracking ice

and olivine.

I reach out a desperate hand,

fingers grasping your silhouette,

asking, begging,

'Are you there?'

Þögn.

A salty wind picks up,

caressing my bare feet, up my calves,

an invisible hand holds on

as soft and as caring as my mother's voice.

It circles me, up and up

and around and around,

hair aflutter,

and stop.

The air settles,

hands stroking down my body.

Two lips up to the shell of my ear,

'I am.'

A...

I swallow,

'Was it always like this?'

A giggle and another soft tornado,

birch leaves clattering.

Hands grab at my wrists,

lips to my nape, louder,

'*Nei.*'

You leave, wind and leaves

and softness in your wake.

Then grass, waving against my ankles,

and with a wiggle of my toes,

moss beneath my feet.

I push in, spread my arms and breathe,

breathe the cool air,

salty and mossy and earthy and cold.

I open my eyes,

bright sky like violets and poppies.

'Right...'

Ég sé.

Mountains like watercolour paintings,

lilac and tall and proud,

a crown of snow and ice and frost.

'There you are.'

Yes, there you are,

Fjalladrottningin mín,

there you are.

Mighty and mine,

powerful and bright.

'Is this how it was?'

A deep hum like a chuckle,

and a shaking through the ground,

from the soles of my feet

to my eyes.

'Sometimes.'

She says.

Ég heyri.

The lady of the mountain pushes,

and I tumble back,

into a bed of moss,

under a dancing sky.

Ísafold bestows me with a hug,

berries and sorrel and avens tangled into me.

'And this?'

I sit up, the pinks and greens swirling in the sky,

now a crackling fire before me,

rock as black as mink eyes beneath my feet.

Fields of moss and rock and grass before me,

shining in the pinks and greens of the sky,

glowing with the golden embers of the fire.

Frón stands before me,

the fire a soft roar,

a calming growl.

I gasp silently,

'Is this it?'

He smirks,

pop,

'At times.'

Ég finn.

Frón presses down on my chest

into the moss,

the darkness.

The warmth turns into cold,

stabbing, petrifying,

strong.

I land on you,

Klakinn a tickle of ice up my spine,

starts winking above in the eternal navy.

Kisses upon my skin,

fingers, wrists, elbows, shoulders...

shivers.

I yelp,

'This?'

An intense stare,

through the blues of my eyes,

Jökulmær lips upon my navel.

'Maybe.'

You mumble onto my sternum.

Ég skil.

The glacier princess crushes me,

dripping, melting,

salt.

She releases me into the sea,

drifting, sinking,

I wake.

A deep humming, rumbling within my chest,

through my bones, the stones, the ores.

My skin is yours,

but your mind is mine.

I finally breathe

and you fill me.

I kick and grab and claw,

Skerið grabs onto my feet and pushes,

up, up, up,

I emerge,

bowing before you,

arriving Eylenda.

Ég man.

Afterword

I was born Icelandic, from Icelandic parents from Icelandic families from Icelandic towns. Generations of rough-swearing, tobacco-snorting, salt-crunching sailors, an ancestry of liquorice-chewing, liquor-chugging Vikings that were no longer Vikings. A country of ice and fire and moss, a city of vapour and silvery s's, a home in the shape of a green flounder where I came to be.

I, we, left for warmer lands five years later. Saying goodbye to a land of rich folktales where elves and trolls still dwell in hiding, an earth so wise and magical it haunted and taunted me in dreams, like lost songs and memories that were no longer mine, or never were. Spain welcomed me as a house, but Iceland remained as a lost home. Or so I thought.

The Canaries had their own folktales and earth, wealthy with knowledge and a sense of home...

and then it was home, and Iceland was just another home far away from home, and Spain was also a home far away from home. There, I also came to be, more. Spain gifted me with culture and family and friends, but Iceland sat in the north, never quiet or dormant yet never loud or adamant, ever waiting, smiling, singing.

I abandoned Spain too, twelve years later, found a home away from home away from home, and the giant's singing in the north was joined with warm giggles in the south. And yes, I missed the lands that I call homes, but more than that, I missed my real homes. I missed those that made Iceland a great country of peace and folktales and magic, and those that made Spain a place of calm and culture and happiness. I missed the me that I become there and here and there.

But, through it all, through all the new homes I have come to find, Iceland will always be my first home, because Iceland is the people I learned to love first, and those people, my family and friends and me, are Iceland.

Iceland with its moss and fire, fishing and farming, liquorice and tobacco, folktales and magic... home, my Queen of the Mountain, my country of the north, my Lady of the Ice, my skerry, my island, Eylenda.

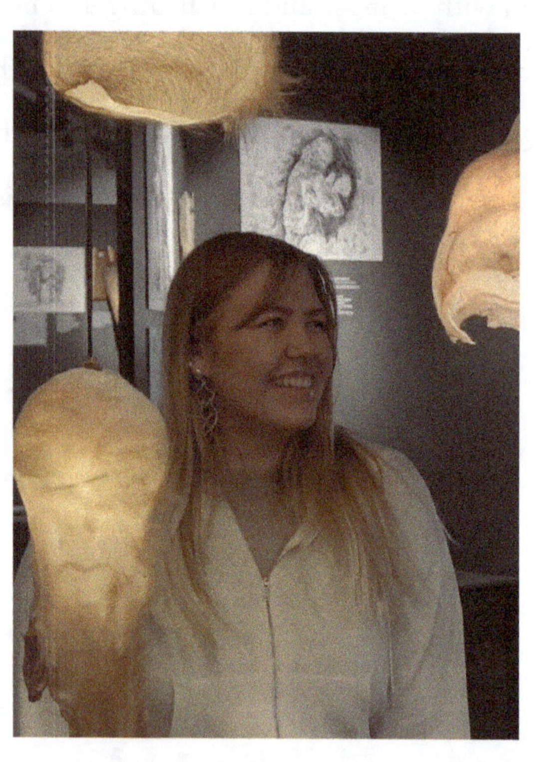

About the Author

Aríel Bertelsen is an Icelandic author and poet, with a passion for writing fantasy and young adult fiction in long-form, short-form, and poetry. Her writing often shows themes around, surrealism, folklore and mythology, nature, and queerness.

She was born in Reykjavík, Iceland, but grew up in Tenerife, Spain. Later on, she moved to the United Kingdom to go to university. She graduated from Kingston University with an undergraduate in English and Creative Writing and is set to graduate with a master's degree in Publishing through the release of this book.